LEADERS LIKE US

Ketanji Brown
JACKSON

BY J.P. MILLER

ILLUSTRATED BY
DAVID WILKERSON

Rourke™

BEFORE AND DURING READING ACTIVITIES

Before Reading: *Building Background Knowledge and Vocabulary*

Building background knowledge can help children process new information and build upon what they already know. Before reading a book, it is important to tap into what children already know about the topic. This will help them develop their vocabulary and increase their reading comprehension.

Questions and Activities to Build Background Knowledge:

1. Look at the front cover of the book and read the title. What do you think this book will be about?
2. What do you already know about this topic?
3. Take a book walk and skim the pages. Look at the table of contents, photographs, captions, and bold words. Did these text features give you any information or predictions about what you will read in this book?

Vocabulary: *Vocabulary Is Key to Reading Comprehension*

Use the following directions to prompt a conversation about each word.

- Read the vocabulary words.
- What comes to mind when you see each word?
- What do you think each word means?

Vocabulary Words:
- court
- data
- debate
- evidence
- judge
- justice
- nomination
- oratory

During Reading: *Reading for Meaning and Understanding*

To achieve deep comprehension of a book, children are encouraged to use close reading strategies. During reading, it is important to have children stop and make connections. These connections result in deeper analysis and understanding of a book.

 Close Reading a Text

During reading, have children stop and talk about the following:

- Any confusing parts
- Any unknown words
- Text to text, text to self, text to world connections
- The main idea in each chapter or heading

Encourage children to use context clues to determine the meaning of any unknown words. These strategies will help children learn to analyze the text more thoroughly as they read.

When you are finished reading this book, turn to the next-to-last page for **Text-Dependent Questions** and an **Extension Activity**.

TABLE OF CONTENTS

ALL RISE!

Are you a good listener? Have you ever helped friends or family solve a problem? Ketanji Brown Jackson makes sure people in her **court** are treated fairly. She is an associate **justice** for the Supreme Court of the United States. She is a leader in government.

The room was filled with reporters. President Joe Biden had just announced Ketanji Brown Jackson as his pick for the Supreme Court. When he ran for office, he promised voters he would choose a Black woman justice if given the chance. She would be the first. President Biden said, "For too long our government, our courts haven't looked like America." He was right! This was a historic moment.

SUPREME COURT JUSTICES

The Supreme Court is part of the executive branch of government. Once nominated by the president and confirmed by the Senate, a Supreme Court justice serves a lifetime. There are nine justices. One chief justice and eight associate justices.

Ketanji stood proud and accepted the **nomination**. She was ready for the job. But first, she had to be voted in by the US Senate. If approved, she would join three other women on the Supreme Court. She would be the third African American in the court's history.

WHAT DOES THE COURT LOOK LIKE?

Of the 115 Supreme Court justices to have served before Ketanji Brown Jackson, 108 were White men, five were women, and two have been African American.

A STAR IN THE MAKING

Books and papers littered the kitchen table. Every night Ketanji's father studied there. Both of Ketanji's parents were public school teachers. But her father went back to school to become a lawyer. Ketanji admired her father. She sat next to him doing her own schoolwork—coloring. When she grew up, she wanted to become a lawyer too.

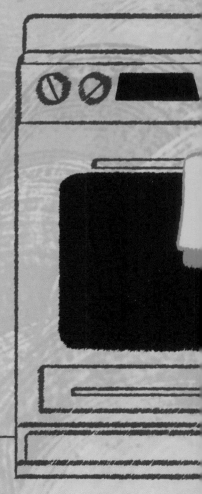

Ketanji was a great student in high school. She was a star in the making. Her classmates thought so too! They elected her as student body president.

The idea of an intense discussion excited Ketanji. So, she joined the **debate** team. In 1988, she competed with students across the nation in a contest where they wrote and gave original speeches. Ketanji won and became a national **oratory** champion.

The Miami Palmetto Senior High School debate team helped prepare Ketanji for a career in law. She said she "learned how to reason and how to write." It was the confidence builder she needed.

Ketanji left Miami, Florida, for Harvard University that fall. She studied government. It was a stepping-stone to becoming a **judge**. After she graduated, Ketanji worked for *Time* magazine. She was a staff reporter and researcher. She loved digging up information. She combed through files and **data**. It got her ready for long hours researching laws.

HLS

HARVARD LAW

Before she knew it, she was back at Harvard, this time Harvard Law School. In high school, Ketanji told her guidance counselor about her goal of going to Harvard. Her counselor said she shouldn't set her sights so high. Ketanji not only attended Harvard twice, but also graduated with honors both times!

Most judges will work as lawyers before they become a judge. Many of them will act as lawyers for big companies. Ketanji chose a different path.

She knew that many Americans could not afford lawyers for court. When someone can't afford a lawyer, the government assigns them a public defender so they can still have a fair trial. She decided to work as one. She is the first justice to have served as a federal public defender.

HERE COMES THE JUDGE

Before long, Ketanji was working as a judge. "All rise!" the bailiff would shout. She'd hit the wooden gavel on the bench and say, "Court is now in session!" She was making a name for herself.

She was always prepared for court...
...stood firm in the law...
...and made fair decisions.

One of those decisions was when the meat industry took the United States Department of Agriculture (USDA) to court. They did not want to show customers where their meat came from. Ketanji let both sides give their **evidence**. She ruled in favor of the USDA. Now, meat in US grocery stores has the country of origin on the label.

Before Ketanji could become a Supreme Court justice, she had to have a confirmation hearing. The Senate asked her a lot of questions. She answered them all as best she could. Her daughter Leila beamed with pride as she looked on.

Leila knew her mother was perfect for the job. She even wrote President Barack Obama a letter saying so when she was 11 years old. She wanted President Obama to consider her mother for the Supreme Court. She described her mother as being a loyal, a determined, and an honest person. Nearly six years later, Leila's dream for her mother came true.

On April 7, 2022, the Senate confirmed Judge Ketanji Brown Jackson as a Supreme Court justice. This moment solidified Ketanji Brown Jackson's place in American history as the first Black woman to serve on the Supreme Court. She is married to her college sweetheart, Dr. Patrick G. Jackson. The couple and their two daughters, Leila and Talia, live in Washington, DC.

> **The United States of America is the greatest beacon of hope in democracy the world has ever known.**
>
> –Ketanji Brown Jackson

TIME LINE

1970   Ketanji is born Ketanji Onyika Brown on September 14th to Johnny and Ellery Brown in Washington, DC, but grows up in Miami, Florida.

1988   Ketanji graduates from Miami Palmetto Senior High School. She wins the Grand National Tournament and becomes a National Oratory Champion.

1988   Ketanji starts college at Harvard University, majoring in government.

1992   Ketanji graduates magna cum laude from Harvard Law School.

1992-93   Ketanji works as a staff recorder and researcher for *Time* magazine.

1996   Ketanji marries heart surgeon Dr. Patrick G. Jackson.

1999   Ketanji clerks for Justice Stephen Breyer.

2005-07   Ketanji works as an assistant public defender in Washington, DC.

2009   President Barack Obama nominates Ketanji to become Vice Chair of the US Sentencing Committee. The Senate confirms unanimously in 2010.

2013   Ketanji is the judge for the American Meat Institute v. The US Department of Agriculture case.

2016   Eleven-year-old Leila Jackson writes a letter to President Obama requesting he replace Justice Antonin Scalia with her mother.

2022   Ketanji is confirmed as the 116th Supreme Court justice.

GLOSSARY

court (kort): a place where legal cases are presented and decided

data (DAY-tuh): information that is collected so that something can be done with it

debate (di-BATE): a discussion in which people express different opinions

evidence (EV-i-duhns): information that helps prove if something is true or not true

judge (juhj): the person who is in charge in a court of law and decides on the matters brought to court

justice (JUHS-tis): a judge

nomination (NAH-muh-nay-shuhn): the process of suggesting that someone would be good for an important job

oratory (OR-uh-tor-ee): the art of public speaking in an effective way

INDEX

TEXT-DEPENDENT QUESTIONS

1. Why did President Joe Biden decide to nominate a Black woman for the Supreme Court?

2. Where did Ketanji go to law school?

3. What has to appear on the label of all meat in US grocery stores?

4. What high school activity helped boost Ketanji's confidence?

5. Who wrote to President Obama saying Ketanji would make a good Supreme Court justice?

EXTENSION ACTIVITY

With friends, family members, or classmates, conduct a mock trial. First, choose your case. It could be from a movie, show, or story. Was Humpty Dumpty's fall an accident? Is the wolf in *The Three Little Pigs* guilty? Then, select the judge, lawyers, defendant, plaintiff, and jury. Allow lawyers to present evidence and question witnesses. The jury will discuss and vote on a decision. The judge will maintain order in the court and decide sentencing.

ABOUT THE AUTHOR

J. P. Miller is able to bring little- and well-known people and events in African American history to life for young readers through her gift of storytelling. She is particularly excited that her *Leaders Like Us* series has been such a success with readers and educators. J.P. is also the author of *Careers in the US Military* and *Black Stories Matter*. She is the winner of the 2021 Black Authors Matter Award sponsored by the National Black Book Festival. J.P. lives in metro Atlanta and enjoys playing pickleball and swimming in her spare time.

ABOUT THE ILLUSTRATOR

David Wilkerson was born in Denver, CO and is currently based in Maryland. He developed a love for illustration during his high school years. His career began in the animation industry, working as a character designer, prop designer, and background designer. He has worked as a designer on projects for: Hulu, Cartoon Network, Springhill Company, FOX Sports, and FUSE. He believes that there is healing in storytelling, and that it is the job of creatives to contribute to that cause.

© 2023 Rourke Educational Media

www.rourkebooks.com

PHOTO CREDITS: page 20: Fred Schilling, Collection of the Supreme Court of the United St/picture alliance / Consolidated News Photos/Newscom

Quote source: ABC News, "Judge Ketanji Brown Jackson poised to make Supreme Court history," YouTube video, 8:45, February 26, 2022, https://www.youtube.com/watch?v=iel3ADsimGE.

Edited by: Hailey Scragg
Illustrations by: David Wilkerson
Cover and interior layout by: J.J. Giddings

Library of Congress PCN Data

Ketanji Brown Jackson / J.P. Miller
(Leaders Like Us)
ISBN 978-1-73165-629-2 (hard cover)
ISBN 978-1-73165-602-5 (soft cover)
ISBN 978-1-73165-611-7 (e-book)
ISBN 978-1-73165-620-9 (e-pub)
Library of Congress Control Number: 2022941694

Rourke Educational Media
Printed in the United States of America
01-3152211937